Hiring the Best

Hiring the Best

ANN M. McGILL

The Business Skills Express Series

BUSINESS ONE IRWIN/MIRROR PRESS
Homewood, IL 60430
Boston, MA 02116

© RICHARD D. IRWIN, INC., 1994

Mirror Press: David R. Helmstadter
                                 Carla F. Tishler

Editor-in-chief: Jeffrey A. Krames
Project editor: Stephanie M. Britt
Production manager: Diane Palmer
Designer: Jeanne M. Rivera
Art coordinator: Heather Burbridge
Illustrator: Boston Graphics, Inc.
Compositor: TCSystems, Inc.
Typeface: 12/14 Criterion
Printer: Malloy Lithographing, Inc.

Library of Congress Cataloging-in-Publication Data

McGill, Ann M.
    Hiring the best / Ann M. McGill.
        p.   cm.—(Business skills express)
    ISBN 1-55623-865-7
    1. Employment interviewing.   2. Employee selection.   I. Title.
II. Series.
HF5549.5.I6M326   1994
658.9'11—dc20   93-4

Printed in the United States of America
1 2 3 4 5 6 7 8 9 0 ML 0 9 8 7 6 5 4 3

PREFACE

This book is for you: if you have been puzzled when the ideal candidate only lasted three months on the job; if you have been disappointed when a pleasant personality failed to perform; if you have been intimidated by an aggressive candidate; if you have found yourself tongue-tied when interviewing. This book will help you improve your interviewing skills and enable you to select better employees.

Effective interviewing increases your success in choosing a job candidate who best fits your job requirements and your company's environment. Enhancing your interviewing techniques increases your professional communication skills and prevents costly hiring errors.

This book presents a complete hiring process with supporting procedures that will enhance your employee selection. Each chapter contains useful examples and practical techniques that you can use in all of your hiring interviews.

How can you get the most from this book? First, complete the self-assessment. Pay particular attention to your "almost never" responses and identify those areas where you need the most support.

Once completed, this book can be used as a reference whenever you are facing a new employee hire. The Skill Maintenance checklist on the back inside cover can be used to ensure that you practice all the techniques for a successful hire.

Ann M. McGill

ABOUT THE AUTHOR

Ann M. McGill, president of McGill Enterprises, provides personnel administration and recruiting support services to a wide range of businesses including banks, hospitals, resorts, and the food service industry. She has over 15 years experience in human resources management. In her consulting practice, Ms. McGill specializes in helping employers solve and prevent employee problems, developing employee potential through training and coaching, and designing systems and policies to support business goals.

ABOUT
BUSINESS ONE IRWIN

Business One Irwin is the nation's premier publisher of business books. As a Times Mirror company, we work closely with Times Mirror training organizations, including Zenger-Miller, Inc., Learning International, Inc., and Kaset International, to serve the training needs of business and industry.

About the Business Skills Express Series

This expanding series of authoritative, concise, and fast-paced books delivers high quality training on key business topics at a remarkably affordable cost. The series will help managers, supervisors, and front line personnel in organizations of all sizes and types hone their business skills while enhancing job performance and career satisfaction.

Business Skills Express books are ideal for employee seminars, independent self-study, on-the-job training, and classroom-based instruction. Express books are also convenient-to-use references at work.

CONTENTS

Self-Assessment

How do you feel about your interviewing skills and the results of your hiring decisions? This simple self-assessment may confirm your confidence or suggest areas for improvement.

	Almost Always	Sometimes	Almost Never
1. I feel confident that I can conduct a comprehensive hiring interview.	_____	_____	_____
2. I develop job skills criteria for my job openings before I begin.	_____	_____	_____
3. I select applicants to interview who match my job criteria.	_____	_____	_____
4. I understand the employment laws that affect hiring.	_____	_____	_____
5. I do not ask questions that can be construed as discriminatory.	_____	_____	_____
6. I prepare a list of questions in advance of the interview.	_____	_____	_____
7. I ask probing questions to get all the information I need.	_____	_____	_____
8. I avoid asking single-answer questions.	_____	_____	_____
9. I set the tone and build rapport within the first 30 seconds of the interview.	_____	_____	_____
10. I use several effective listening techniques in each interview.	_____	_____	_____
11. I sell the job and my company.	_____	_____	_____
12. I summarize my interview data to make the best selection.	_____	_____	_____
13. I rate and rank each job candidate.	_____	_____	_____
14. I can defend my hiring decision against charges of discrimination.	_____	_____	_____
15. I begin each hiring process with a well-thought-out plan.	_____	_____	_____

Hiring the Best

CHAPTER

1 | The Interview

This chapter will help you to:

- Analyze an interview case study.
- Evaluate the interview's strengths and weaknesses.

Read the case study carefully. Jot down any of your comments in the Notes column to the right of the dialogue.

THE INTERVIEW CASE STUDY

Marcia LaVoie, manager of administration, is interviewing a candidate, Sara Anderson, for a receptionist/secretary position. Use the page margins to jot down notes on the interview.

Marcia:

[*Standing behind the desk, extends her hand.*] Thank you for coming in. I understand that you know Tom Jacobs, our sales manager.

Sara:

Well, I don't really know him. He's a friend of my parents. He told them about the opening for a secretary.

Marcia:

Please have a seat. Actually, the opening is for a receptionist/secretary. In fact, the position is our front desk. The woman who greeted you will be leaving at the end of the month. We hope to fill the spot before she leaves.

Sara:

Oh! Mr. Jacobs had said a secretarial position. I thought it might be in a department.

Marcia:

No, it is not. And I want to make sure you understand that. Are you still interested in discussing the position?

Sara:

Oh, definitely! My temporary job ends next week. And I need to find a full-time job.

Marcia:

[*Nods.*] All right. Now, let's find out about you. From your résumé, I see that you have secretarial training and experience. I am interested in learning about your work experience, your different job responsibilities—what you liked and what you didn't like. In short, as much as I can. Have you worked in a reception area?

Sara:

Not full-time, but in my first job I did fill in for the receptionist when I was a floater.

Marcia:

I see that the floater job was your first job. What is a floater?

Sara:

It's like an in-house temp. I got my assignments from personnel. Basically, I filled in for anyone who was out.

Marcia:

I see. Whom did that include?

Sara:

Mostly, the secretaries. I also filled in for the receptionist, the switchboard, and the mailroom.

Marcia:

As the fill-in, what did you do?

Sara:

I typed all the correspondence, answered the telephones, took messages, made appointments. In marketing, I set up the rooms for meetings. I learned how to set up all the multimedia equipment. I also produced the sales reports and any other reports that they needed.

Marcia:

Now, according to your résumé, after that position, you were a customer service clerk.

Sara:

Yes. After three months, I could apply for another job in the company. The customer service job was the first one to come along. So I went for that one. It was mostly a data entry job.

Marcia:

You don't sound very enthusiastic about that job.

Sara:

It really wasn't what I wanted to do. I got a degree in secretarial sciences and I wanted to be an executive secretary. I did more secretarial work as a floater.

Marcia:

Why did you apply for the customer service job?

Sara:

I thought it would be a stepping-stone to another job. I liked being a floater, but it was considered a low job and no one stayed a floater for long.

Marcia:

I see. After the customer service position, you changed companies. What happened?

Sara:

> I wasn't going anywhere in customer service. Most of the people in the department were a lot older and had been in those jobs a long time. A friend of mine worked at the travel agency and told me about a job there. So I went down for an interview and got the job.

Marcia:

> When you interviewed for that position, did you feel it offered you the opportunities you were looking for, or was it just an escape?

Sara:

> The way the owner described the job sounded like it was very close to an administrative-assistant-type position. And that would match my educational background. So I was very glad to get the job.

Marcia:

> You're smiling now. This job appealed to you?

Sara:

> Yes, I loved it. I was given a lot of responsibility right away. I opened up the agency every morning. I handled all the incoming calls for the travel consultants. I typed all the correspondence for the owner, Mrs. Caldwell, who was a terrific boss.

Marcia:

> In what way was she a terrific boss?

Sara:

> Mrs. Caldwell made it a point to say something to all of us each day. She was very positive and a great teacher.

Marcia:

> How was the way she treated you different from how you were treated at the other company?

Sara:

> The people at the other company were more status-oriented. If your job wasn't important, neither were you. I didn't like that.

Marcia:

> I don't blame you. I wouldn't want to feel that what I did wasn't important. Were you treated that way by everyone in the company?

Sara:

> No. It was mainly by my supervisor. I don't think she liked me.

Marcia:

> Why do you feel that she didn't like you?

Sara:

I don't know. I got my work done on time. Other people liked me all right. I don't know what it was about her.

Marcia:

If I were to ask any of your supervisors to describe you, what would they tell me?

Sara:

All of them would say I was a hard worker, that I got along with everyone, and would help anyone who needed help. I was always on time. Mrs. Caldwell would say I was well groomed—although, at first, that's not what she said!

Marcia:

Oh, why was that?

Sara:

I guess I was a little too casual. That's where she was different. She talked to me about it and told me what she expected for dress code.

Marcia:

If I understand you correctly, your dress style was more suited to, say, going out with your friends than going to work?

Sara:

That's right. My clothes were neat and trendy but not for business.

Marcia:

[*Nods.*] Why did you stop working at the travel agency? That was about three months ago.

Sara:

Yes, Mrs. Caldwell got sick and closed the agency. I didn't know what to do next, so I went to a temp agency and have been working in different companies.

Marcia:

I heard you say that you opened the travel agency in the morning. One of the duties of this position is to open the office and let employees into the building. How did Mrs. Caldwell rate your reliability in this area?

Sara:

Mrs. Caldwell would tell you I never missed a day and that I was always on time. I guess she would give me a good rating.

Marcia:

You are currently working, correct?

Sara:

Yes, I have been working as a temporary at a manufacturing plant. I do a lot of data entry, filing, and typing reports. But the woman I replaced is coming back from maternity leave, so I will be out of work again.

Marcia:

How do you like working in manufacturing?

Sara:

I was surprised. It is really pretty interesting. And the people there are very friendly.

Marcia:

Hmmmm. If you could write your own job description right now, what would you want to include in your new job?

Sara:

I think I want a job where I have my own responsibilities. I would want to use my educational background, so I would want typing, working on computers, producing reports. I like numbers. I think I would want something to do with accounting.

Marcia:

That's interesting. I don't think I heard you mention accounting in any of your positions. Did you work with numbers in any of these jobs?

Sara:

I am working with numbers right now at the plant and I like doing the reports. My highest grades at school were in accounting.

Marcia:

Now might be a good time to tell me about your education program.

Sara:

It was an excellent program. We really covered everything—typing, dictation, word processing, office management, marketing, personnel, and communications, including letter writing. I took accounting because I did well in math.

Marcia:

Your program sounds very comprehensive. You mentioned that you did well in math. What other courses did you do well in?

Sara:

I did well in all my courses. I had a B+ average overall. The only course I got a C in was marketing and that was because I didn't like the teacher.

Marcia:

I see. How did your education help you on your jobs?

Sara:

All my jobs have required computers and typing. So those courses really prepared me the best.

Marcia:

What didn't your education prepare you for?

Sara:

Dealing with all the different personalities. I think my first job opened my eyes. I don't think I handled some situations very well. But that changed once I changed companies.

Marcia:

Sara, you have given me a very good picture of yourself. I want you to tell me why you think you would be a good candidate for our opening here.

Sara:

Well, I have experience dealing with the public. I enjoy working with people. I am well organized. I can get work out quickly. I am good on the telephone with customers.

Marcia:

As I indicated, this is not a straight secretarial position. How do you feel about this job in light of your career goals?

Sara:

If I'm honest, I say it's not the perfect job. But I have heard good things about your company. I think that it's important to work for a good company. I could have stayed at the travel job forever. The people were great.

Marcia:

Thank you for your directness. Now, do you have any questions for me?

Sara:

How soon will you be making a decision?

1

Marcia:

You are the last one that I will interview. I will be reviewing all of my interviews. I will make a decision by the end of the week.

Sara:

I am making $7 an hour as a temporary.

Marcia:

$7 is in our pay range. This position does come with benefits. I will give you a summary of our benefits to take with you. Anything else?

Sara:

No, I don't think so. I hope to hear from you.

Marcia:

You will, one way or the other. It's been nice talking to you, Sara. Thank you for coming in to see me.

CASE STUDY EVALUATION

Would You Hire Sara Anderson?

1. Do you have enough information to make a hiring decision?

_____

2. In your opinion, what experience and skills does Sara possess that match the job?

_____
_____
_____

3. Would you hire Sara for this position? Why or why not?

_____
_____
_____
_____

4. What are Sara's strengths?

_____
_____
_____

5. What are Sara's weaknesses?

_____
_____
_____

How Well Was the Interview Conducted?

Before the interview, Marcia jotted down some notes about what she wanted to learn from each of the job candidates:

> From each candidate I want to learn the following:
>
> Real interest in the job?
>
> Education?
>
> Work experience?
>
> Punctuality? Attendance?
>
> Getting along with others . . . all ages, types?
>
> Career oriented . . . or content with routine job?

1. Did Marcia get answers to all her questions from the interview with Sara? List the answered questions from her notes.

_____
_____
_____
_____

2. Summarize what Marcia learned about Sara.

_____
_____
_____
_____

3. What were the most effective questions that Marcia asked? Why were they effective?

_____
_____
_____
_____
_____
_____
_____

4. What questions would you have asked Sara that Marcia did not?

_____
_____
_____

1

Rating Marcia

What is your overall rating of Marcia as an interviewer?

Poor   Good   Very Good   Excellent

What could Marcia do to improve her rating as an interviewer?

_____

_____

_____

YOUR INTERVIEW GOALS

Like Marcia, you will want to get certain information from each candidate whom you interview. Before you begin interviewing:

- Make sure you know the particulars of the job (main tasks, hours, environment, and special duties).
- Recognize the kinds of work experience that candidates may have that will be similar to your job opening.
- Determine the educational or training needs of the job.
- Consider what work habits will be important for the successful candidate to possess.
- Think about the kind of motivation the candidate needs to do the job successfully.

Once you have imagined the ideal candidate, jot down the important points you need to learn from each candidate.

From every candidate I want to learn:

_____

_____

_____

_____

_____

In the next several chapters, you will work on skills to help you hire the right candidates for your job openings. The chapters will explore all aspects of a four-part plan to successful hiring, as outlined here.

Four-Part Plan to Successful Hiring

1. Assessment

    Assess your job opening.

    Describe all the duties and tasks of the job.

    Determine the skills it takes to do the job.

    Identify the experiences you will look for.

    Match the résumés with your selected criteria.

2. Preparation

    Prepare yourself for interviews.

    Know your legal responsibilities.

    Create an effective interview format.

    Develop a list of questions to ask each candidate.

3. Interview

    Conduct a professional and complete interview without interruptions.

    Arrange to have calls and visitors handled.

    Take notes during the interview.

    Provide each candidate with information about the company.

    Sell the position and the company at the end of the interview.

4. Evaluation

    Assess all the candidates' strengths and weaknesses before you make a decision.

    Match each candidate's credentials to the job requirements.

    Complete a comparison chart.

    Check references.

    Select the best candidate.

2 Job Assessment

This chapter will help you to:

- Identify the needed job skills for your job opening.
- Complete a must-have worksheet.
- Identify preferred skills and personal qualities of applicants.
- Review applications and résumés for appropriate criteria.

"WE HAVE AN OPENING"

ATTENTION CHEMISTS !

BS Chemist Requires motivated chemist with high energy level to do process chemistry and isotope synthesis. Must have solid lab and analytical skills. Experience with NMR preferred. New graduates encouraged to apply.

QC Technician QC specialist for high purity NMR solvent manufacturing group. BS or MS in chemistry. One to three years of experience in operation of NMR and other analytical systems preferred. New graduates will be considered.

Jacob Rubinstein, a hiring manager, is frustrated as he sorts through the stack of résumés received in response to the ad. He is having difficulty sorting them. Most applicants are recent graduates with some practical lab experience.

As Jacob reviews the résumés, he realizes that he wants more experience and education for the QC job. None of the résumés seem to have strong enough credentials for the job. The QC technician position requires advanced work and a minimum of three years' lab experience. Jacob now regrets that he was not more specific in the ad. He will have to run another ad to get the kind of candidates he wants. ■

Questions to Consider

1. What basic requirements are the same for both chemist positions?

   _____

   _____

   _____

2. Why would recent graduates feel that they might qualify for the QC technician position?

   _____

   _____

   _____

3. In developing the ad, what could Jacob have done differently to clarify the distinctions between the requirements for each position?

   _____

   _____

   _____

4. Rewrite the QC technician ad.

   _____

   _____

   _____

   _____

To attract candidates with the right credentials, you must first:

- Define the main tasks and special duties of the job.
- Identify what a candidate must have to be considered for the job.
- Select personal or preferred attributes that may make performing the job easier or more effective.

Then you begin reviewing applications, sorting potential candidates for interviews, and interviewing candidates who match your preselected criteria.

If Jacob had completed a must-have worksheet before he placed his ad, he might have developed better ad copy and attracted the right type of candidate. The following is the must-have worksheet that Jacob should have completed before writing and placing his ad.

Must-Have Worksheet

Job Title: QC Technician

Main Purpose of the Job:
To verify purity of chemical products before shipping to customers.

Main Job Tasks:	**Candidate Must Have:**
1. Perform advanced analysis.	**1.** M.S. in Chemistry.
2. Identify problems.	**2.** Three years' experience NMR.
3. Liaison with production.	**3.** Detail orientation.

Preferred (but Not Vital) Skills:
Experience with a variety of analytical systems.

Personal Attributes:
Highly accurate.
Able to handle volume and routine.

JOB/SKILLS MATCH EXERCISE

The key to selecting the right candidates is to identify the skills that match the job requirements. This exercise tests your ability to identify skills for each job task listed.

For each job task below, identify the required skills needed to perform the job successfully.

Task	Required Skills
Example:	
Assemble a probe card using microscope.	Excellent hand-eye coordination.
1. Cash a large volume of checks daily.	_____ _____
2. Solve customer billing problems.	_____ _____
3. Supervise five computer programmers.	_____ _____
4. Coordinate production of monthly financial reports.	_____ _____
5. Distribute mail to home office personnel.	_____ _____
6. Process claims payments using computer terminal.	_____ _____
7. Sell the top-of-the-line cosmetics.	_____ _____
8. Purchase office supplies.	_____ _____

To complete your own must-have worksheet, consider the following questions:

Main Job Tasks

1. What is the main purpose?
2. What are the essential duties?
3. What are the main priorities?
4. With whom will this candidate interact?
5. What deadlines does this job have?
6. What equipment does this job use?

Must-Have Requirements

1. What basic skill requirements must the candidate have?
2. What special skills should a candidate have?

3. What kind of experience should a candidate have?

4. How much experience is needed? (One month? One year?)

5. What level of education is needed?

Preferred/Personal Skills

1. How much stamina is required?

2. What work characteristics are important? (Ability to work unsupervised? Manual dexterity? Detail orientation?)

3. What level of communication skills is needed?

4. How long would you like a person to remain in this position?

5. What additional requirements are preferred, but not mandatory?

Complete a must-have worksheet for a position in your department.

Must-Have Worksheet

Job Title:

Main Purpose of the Job:

Main Job Tasks:	**Candidate Must Have:**
1.	1.
2.	2.
3.	3
4.	4.
5.	5.

Preferred (but Not Vital) Skills:

Personal Attributes:

2

Must-Have Worksheet

Job Title: Receptionist/Secretary

Main Purpose of the Job:
To answer the switchboard and greet visitors.

Main Job Tasks:	**Candidate Must Have:**
1. To operate the multiline switchboard and direct calls courteously.	1. Six months' switchboard experience. Clear and distinct communication skills.
2. To greet and sign in visitors and alert appropriate personnel.	2. Able to meet and greet the public with courtesy at all times.
3. To sort and distribute mail; to send and receive express packages.	3. Able to handle details.
4. To provide typing support to four departments.	4. Accurate typing skills. Letter/memo experience.
5. To complete special typing and collation projects for a variety of departments.	

Preferred (but Not Vital) Skills:
1. One to two years working in an office environment.

Personal Attributes:
1. Able to work unsupervised.
2. Able to organize and prioritize work.
3. Always pleasant.

CASE STUDY: REVIEW APPLICATIONS AND RÉSUMÉS

Look at the must-have worksheet that Marcia LaVoie, the hiring manager from Chapter 1, completed before she began her interviews. You will also find two of the résumés she received. Review both the worksheet and the résumés. Jot down your observations about each candidate, based on her résumé. Answer the questions that follow the résumés.

2

Résumé 10

Martha Wagstaff
3 Summer Street #4; Winston, MD 21044
(301) 790-2369

EDUCATION

1989 Associate Degree in Business
Winston Community College

EXPERIENCE

Winston Electric Company; 10 Burroughs Street;
Winston, MD

Switchboard Operator   Responsible for handling all calls for Electric Company.
Direct calls. Take messages.
(January 1990 to present)

Winston Community College; Fort Hill Road;
Winston, MD

Office Assistant   Responsible for typing and filing for the English department.
Answered telephones. Assisted students.
Part-time. (September 1988–June 1989)

Village House; Main Street; Court, MD

Waitress   Responsible for customer service, cash handling, and training waitresses.
(June 1988 to present)

REFERENCES UPON REQUEST

Write your comments regarding this résumé:

_____
_____
_____
_____
_____
_____
_____
_____
_____
_____

2

Résumé 43

SARA ANDERSON
14 Tolland Road
Winston, MD 21044
(301) 790-2221

OBJECTIVE: To obtain an executive secretarial position.

EDUCATION

1990 Oberlon Junior College
Associate Degree: Secretarial Science

EXPERIENCE

Around the World Travel; High Street; Columbia, MD

3/91–3/92 **Office Assistant** Provided secretarial support to agency president and travel consultants. Handled and directed all incoming calls. Assisted with customer service problems.

6/90–2/91 **United Life Companies; Industrial Way Building 4; Columbia, MD**

9/90–2/91 **Customer Service Clerk** Processed customer payments. Resolved customer problems.

6/90–9/90 **Floater** Provided temporary secretarial support to departments as needed. Provided assistance to the word processing department and the mailroom.

Write your comments regarding this résumé:

_____
_____
_____
_____
_____
_____
_____
_____
_____
_____
_____
_____
_____
_____
_____
_____

■ C a s e   S t u d y   Q u e s t i o n s

1. Using the résumés, match the five job skill requirements with each candidate.

2

Must-Have Requirements	Martha	Sara
Six months' switchboard experience. Clear and distinct communication skills. Able to meet and greet public with courtesy at all times. Able to handle details. Accurate typing skills. Letter/memo experience. **Preferred** One to two years working in an office environment.		

2. On paper, which candidate is the most qualified for the position? Why?

_____

_____

_____

3. While each candidate may not have the precise job/skill experience, each may have transferable skills. What transferable skills does each possess?

_____

_____

_____

4. From the résumés, what are each candidate's personal attributes?

_____

_____

_____

Chapter Checkpoints

Reviewing Résumés

✓ Examine each résumé for completeness, accuracy, and spelling.

✓ Look for gaps between employment dates or for frequent job changes.

✓ Review the job history for progress in terms of responsibilities.

✓ Look for relevant experience and/or comparable experience.

✓ Note the length of time in each job position.

✓ After reading the résumé, you should quickly be able to summarize the candidate's job history clearly and succinctly.

CHAPTER

3 | Legal Notes

This chapter will help you to:

- Identify discriminatory interview questions.
- Reframe interview questions that suggest bias.
- Interview persons with disabilities.
- Prevent discrimination through interview preparation.

RECOGNIZING DISCRIMINATION

A young, successful vice president for a fast-track entrepreneurial firm was conducting a second interview with a woman for a marketing position in his division. The woman has 20 years of experience—more than the hiring manager. After briefing her on his perspective of the company's future, he hesitated, then said: "I know that I am not supposed to ask this, but . . . how do you feel about working for someone younger than you?" The woman acknowledged that his question was an illegal one. However, she responded by stating that she had no problem with the situation. For the next 10 minutes, they discussed the differences in age and experience. ■

If this woman does not receive a job offer from the company, how has the vice president jeopardized his company?

_____
_____
_____
_____
_____
_____
_____
_____

What action can the woman take?

_____

_____

_____

If this woman receives and accepts a job offer from the company, is the company free from future legal action by the woman?

_____

_____

_____

The vice president in the preceding example knew that asking a direct question about age was illegal. Age is one of the areas protected by the Equal Employment Opportunity Act.

Like the vice president, you may not ask questions directed at a job candidate's:

- Race.
- Color.
- Religion.
- Sex.
- National origin.
- Age.
- Marital status.
- Disability.
- Status as a Vietnam-era veteran.

Laws directing your role in the hiring interview continue to mount. The Americans with Disabilities Act (ADA), passed by Congress in 1990, restricts you from asking questions on disabilities and workers' compensation claims.

Your state may enhance equal employment protection with specific state laws. For example, some states have passed laws that prevent hiring discrimination because of a person's sexual orientation.

While you may not intend to ask discriminatory questions or make statements that suggest bias, the job candidate may interpret your questions as violations of his or her rights. The following 20 questions will test your ability to select nondiscriminatory questions.

Are These Questions Discriminatory?

Read each of the following questions. Circle Y if you consider the question discriminatory. Circle N if you believe you can safely and legally ask the question.

3

Y N   1. Are you planning to have children right away?

Y N   2. What does your husband do for a living?

Y N   3. Do you own your home?

Y N   4. What is your maiden name?

Y N   5. Where do your parents live?

Y N   6. Was English your first language?

Y N   7. What religious holidays do you observe?

Y N   8. Have you ever been arrested?

Y N   9. Are you divorced?

Y N   10. What nationality are you?

Y N   11. Do you have a car?

Y N   12. Did you ever serve in the military?

Y N   13. Have your wages ever been garnished?

Y N   14. What are your hobbies?

Y N   15. What language did you speak as a child?

Y N   16. Do you share an apartment with anyone?

Y N   17. What kinds of problems does being disabled cause you?

Y N   18. Will you mind being the oldest one working here?

Y N   19. Do you think you have the physical strength for the job?

Y N   20. What do you do on Sundays?

Hints

When in Doubt

If the question is not directly related to the job, do not ask it.

What Questions Are Considered Discriminatory?

Direct questions pointed at a job candidate's race, color, national origin, sex, age, marital status, sexual orientation, religion, disability, or status as a Vietnam-era veteran are not permitted.

Questions such as the following may seem like obvious ones to avoid:

What is your race? (race)

Are you divorced? (marital status)

How did you become disabled? (disability)

Did you receive an honorable discharge? (veteran)

But questions that explore areas that support an interviewer's biases or stereotypes may be construed as discriminatory and are not permitted.

The following series of questions may appear to job candidates to be directed at their race, national origin, religion, sex, marital status, age, and so on.

Do you own your home? Do you have a car?
(race/national origin)

What is your maiden name? Where do your parents live?
(race/national origin)

What do you do on Sunday? What groups do you belong to?
(religion)

> All of the questions asked in the previous section, as they were worded, are considered discriminatory and should not be asked.

DISCRIMINATORY INTERVIEWERS

In each of the following scenarios, the interviewer has a bias and harbors a certain stereotype about the job candidate. Read each scene from the perspective of the person being interviewed. Answer the questions at the end of each scene.

Scenario One Carl Sanders, the regional vice president for a retail firm, is interviewing Anita Jones for a store management position. After a quick handshake, he asks her: "How many children do you have, Anita?"

3

"Two," she replies.

"And they are both in grade school?" he continues.

"That's right."

"It must be tough to work and miss their school activities. Of course, this particular position requires day and evening hours. You really have to be available at all times."

"I know, Mr. Sanders. I work varied hours right now."

"I know that you do, Anita. But the responsibilities for the management position are greater than those of your current job. And we really need someone who can handle the load and be on call every minute."

What does Carl fear? _____

_____

What stereotype do his questions suggest? _____

_____

On what basis could Anita file a discrimination complaint?

_____

_____

3

Challenge Question One

What questions can you ask to learn about a candidate's personal restrictions that might interfere with job commitments?

Scenario Two Rita Castigliano, a restaurant manager for an exclusive country club, is interviewing Darren McCallister, a young black teenager, for a busboy position.

"Where do you live, Darren?"

"On Liberty Street."

"Is that the housing project?"

"No. Liberty Street is on the other side of town."

"I see. Do you have a car?"

"No, I don't."

"Well, how do you plan on getting to work?"

"My mother can drive me or I can ride my bike."

"Do you live alone with your mother?"

"No, I live with my mother, my sister, and my grandmother."

"And where is your father?"

"He lives in Springfield."

What is the emphasis of Rita's questions? _____

_____

What stereotype is Rita trying to support through her questions?

_____

_____

What basis does Darren have for a discrimination complaint?

_____

_____

Challenge Question Two

If you want to know if a job candidate can and will get to work on time, what can you ask?

Scenario Three Edward Michaelson is interviewing John Frey for a loan officer position.

"John, as you know, we are a strong community organization. It is important that we are viewed as a positive lending institution and that we attract only the best kind of customers. Are you involved or have you been involved in any controversial organizations?"

"No. I have written the occasional letter to my congressman."

"What did you write to your congressman about?"

3

"Well, I asked him to support prochoice and I wrote in support of gay and lesbian rights."

"You don't consider these controversial?"

"Of course they are. But the letters were written as a citizen, not as a member of a group."

"Let me ask you a frank question, Mr. Frey. Are you gay?"

How did Edward cloak his personal biases? _____

_____

Are Edward's questions related to the job? Why or why not?

_____

_____

What basis does John have for a discrimination complaint?

_____

_____

Challenge Question Three

What can you do to prevent your personal biases from surfacing in an interview?

APPLICANTS WITH DISABILITIES

The Americans with Disabilities Act (ADA) of 1990 states that a qualified person with a disability is one who can perform the essential duties of the job with or without reasonable accommodations, has the requisite skills and experience for the job, and meets other job-related requirements.

When Richard Santiago first started stuffing statements for the bank, his two female co-workers complained to the manager that Richard was a nuisance and did not stay at his desk. The manager knew that the two women resented the mentally handicapped young man. It was hard for them to believe that he could do the same job that they had been doing for years. Unlike the manager, they did not see beyond his disability. Richard not only performed the same job as the women, but he grew in that job and learned additional tasks. Over time, the two women realized that Richard was "able."

Richard, like other disabled persons, has suffered from the subtle discrimination of the nondisabled, who imagine what the disabled cannot do. The intent of the ADA is to challenge the vision of the nondisabled. ■

ADA's Two Key Hiring Points

1. *Determine the requirements for the essential job duties.* (Essential job duties are the primary duties of the position.) Evaluate all candidates with this criteria.

   An entry-level accounting position requires a degree in accounting. You have three candidates, one of whom has a hearing disability. The hiring focus should be on the degree and coursework and not on the hearing loss.

3

2. *Make reasonable accommodations for the person with the diasbility so that he or she can perform the job.*

The candidate with the hearing disability has the best academic record. You decide to hire her. Because answering the phones is a department necessity, you plan to install a special telephone for her.

Vision Test

When you see a person in a wheelchair or a blind man with a white cane or a young woman with Down's syndrome, do you visualize them at work or do you focus on the chair, the cane, and the lines of the eyes?

What Is Essential?

The personnel manager has just posted the switchboard operator's position on the employee bulletin board.

Job Posting

Job Opening: Switchboard Operator

Duties:
    1. Operate switchboard.
    2. Direct calls accurately.
    3. Take complete messages.
    4. Help collate for special projects.
    5. Act as vacation backup for mailroom.

Hours: 7:30 A.M. to 3:00 P.M.

Level 3   Call personnel for interview.

Sandra Chung calls personnel. Sandra has switchboard experience but has a disability that limits her lifting. The mailroom duties include daily heavy package handling. She wants to know if she can still apply for the job.

What should the personnel manager tell her?

_____
_____
_____

What are the essential job duties for the switchboard operator?

_____
_____
_____

What are the marginal job duties? _____
_____
_____

What kinds of adjustments can be made to perform this job?

_____
_____
_____

HOW SHOULD AN APPLICANT WITH A DISABILITY BE INTERVIEWED?

1. Treat the applicant with a disability with the same courtesy and understanding that you use for all of your applicants. Do not patronize.

2. Greet the applicant as you greet all your applicants. Alert the applicant to any actions you are going to take that may not be obvious to that person. For example, tell a blind person: "Let me shake your hand."

3. Give the applicant the same kind of information you give all applicants.

4. Look the applicant in the face. Focus on the person, not the disability.

5. Ask the same questions of the person with a disability as you would a person without a disability.

6. Put yourself and the applicant at ease. Adapt where necessary. For example, give a hearing-impaired applicant your list of questions. This can help reduce your tension as well as the applicant's.

7. Take the vision test again.

3

Questions to Consider

Rewrite the following questions to eliminate bias and to focus on job performance.

Biased	Job-Related
1. Do you mind being the only female in the office?	
2. Have you had previous problems with your accent?	
3. I suppose you want special treatment for your religious holidays?	
4. Do you attribute your good marks in math to being Chinese?	
5. Will your disability prevent you from doing this job?	
6. What was it like growing up in Puerto Rico?	
7. How did you handle your kids when you told them you were getting a divorce?	

Chapter Checkpoints

Avoid Hiring Discrimination

✓ Know who is protected by law and stay up-to-date on legal changes.

✓ Clearly describe the requirements for the job, free from your biases and stereotypes.

✓ Prepare interview questions in advance.

✓ Develop performance-related questions.

✓ Ask each candidate the same questions.

✓ Develop interchangeable questions for males and females.

✓ Recognize your own biases and prejudices. Rework questions that support your stereotypes.

✓ Evaluate job candidates on their qualifications for the job—not their color, accent, home life, religious beliefs, or life-style.

✓ Remember that you represent yourself and your company.

4 | Interview Formats

This chapter will help you to:

- Create interview formats that will let you interview anytime and anywhere.
- Vary your pattern of interview questions.

To begin this chapter, identify your personal goal when interviewing.

The best interview is the one in which I _____

_____

_____

_____

_____.

Your interview has a twofold purpose:

1. To obtain enough information to select the person who best matches the job and who will fit into the company and work well with the other members of your department.
2. To project with accuracy how well the selected individual will perform on the job and in the future.

The best interviews are the ones that result in a long-term, satisfied, and productive employee. Successful interviewers hire the best because they have established tried and true personal interview formats that enable them to get the necessary information from job candidates.

INTERVIEWER PATTERNS

If you have interviewed, you have no doubt established a pattern that feels comfortable to you. Let's examine some typical interviewer patterns.

4

Type	Pattern
All talk	
80% interviewer	The interviewer describes the job, the company, and what his or her preferences are; does most of the talking.
20% job candidate	The job candidate answers few questions; often confirms what the interviewer reads on résumé or assumes from candidate's appearance.
All ears	
10% interviewer	The interviewer opens with "tell me about yourself" and uses nonverbals to encourage the candidate to keep talking.
90% job candidate	The candidate does most of the talking and is expected to keep talking about him- or herself. The interviewer usually signals the close with a short statement.
Equal time	
50% interviewer	The interviewer and the candidate share equal time. The interviewer describes the job and then the candidate responds to questions. The candidate asks questions and the interviewer responds.
50% job candidate	

Your Opinion

1. What is the ideal percentage of time an interviewer spends talking rather than listening?

_____

2. In what instances does the ideal percentage vary?

_____

_____

3. Describe your current interview pattern and your ideal interview pattern.

_____
_____
_____
_____
_____
_____
_____
_____
_____
_____

4. What do you need to do to bring your current interview pattern up to your ideal?

_____

_____

_____

THE INTERVIEW FORMAT

Creating an effective interview format can help you to:

- Control the flow of talk in the interview.
- Obtain enough information from the job candidate.
- Avoid the use of illegal questions.
- Prevent overselling the position.
- Improve your listening skills.
- Present you and your company in a positive light.

Hints ────────────────────────────

If You Interview Often . . .

You will find that an established format enables you to present a professional image to your job candidates and to obtain consistent quality information from them.

Creating an interview format is like composing a letter. An interview consists of three major parts:

1. **The introduction**—You greet and welcome the job candidate, clarify the purpose of the interview, and tell the candidate what to expect in the interview.
2. **The body**—You obtain information about the candidate's job history, education, and personal characteristics through a series of questions.
3. **The closing**—You thank the candidate for the interview; answer any questions; sell the job and the company, if appropriate; and tell the candidate what the next step will be in the hiring process and when a decision will be made.

The Introduction

In the introduction, you establish rapport with the job candidate and set the tone for the interview. In your introduction, you should:

Greet the candidate.

Extend a welcome.

Clarify the purpose of the interview.

State what will happen in the interview.

Review the opening of the case study interview from Chapter 1. (Note: Marcia LaVoie's statements are repeated below and numbered for easy reference.) Does Marcia include all the elements of the introduction? Answer the questions that follow.

Marcia:

[*Standing behind the desk, extends her hand.*] Thank you for coming in. I understand that you know Tom Jacobs, our sales manager.

Sara:

Well, I don't really know him. He's a friend of my parents. He told them about the opening for a secretary.

Marcia:

Please have a seat. Actually, the opening is for a receptionist/secretary. In fact, the position is our front desk. The woman who greeted you will be leaving at the end of the month. We hope to fill the spot before she leaves.

Sara:

Oh! Mr. Jacobs had said a secretarial position. I thought it might be in a department.

Marcia:

No, it is not. And I want to make sure you understand that. Are you still interested in discussing the position?

Sara:

Oh, definitely! My temporary job ends next week. And I need to find a full-time job.

Marcia:

[*Nods.*] All right. Now, let's find out about you. From your résumé, I see that you have secretarial training and experience. I am interested in learning about your work experience, your different job responsibilities—what you liked and what you didn't like. In short, as much as I can. . . .

1. Identify the elements of the introduction that Marcia used in her opening words to Sara.

_____

_____

_____

_____

2. Why did using the elements of the introduction create efficiency for Marcia?

_____

_____

_____

3. What tone did Marcia establish in her introduction to Sara?

_____

_____

4. If you were Marcia, is there anything you would have done differently in the introduction? If so, what?

_____

_____

_____

_____

The Body

The body of the interview is where you get the information you need to make a solid hiring decision. You will want to explore various pertinent areas of experience with each candidate. It is helpful to group these areas together so that you can get a complete picture of the candidate. The three main areas of experience include the job candidate's:

1. **Work experience**
   Job history patterns.
   Growth in responsibilities.
   Skills developed.
   Communication abilities.
   Problem-solving ability.

4

Decision-making ability.

Discretionary skills.

Response to supervision.

Current job duties.

Preferred work environments.

Ability to work with others.

2. **Education**

Formal schooling.

Special trade schools.

Certificate programs.

Internal seminars.

Best grades/worst grades.

Favorite subjects.

School influences.

School deficiencies.

3. **Personal traits**

Work habits.

Personality.

Personal goals.

Motivation.

Strengths/weaknesses.

Personal assessment.

Referring to the case study and your notes from Chapter 1, answer the following questions.

1. What questions did Marcia ask Sara regarding her work experience?

_____

_____

_____

2. What questions did Marcia ask regarding Sara's working relationships with others?

_____

_____

_____

3. What aspects of Sara's education did Marcia focus on?

_____
_____
_____

4. In the course of the interview, how did Marcia uncover Sara's personality and work habits?

_____
_____
_____

5. From the information Marcia obtained, can you describe what motivates Sara?

_____
_____
_____

The Closing

In the closing, give the job candidate the opportunity to ask questions and take the opportunity to sell the job and the company to the candidate, when appropriate. Your closing can include:

Thanking the candidate.

Fielding candidate questions.

Selling the job/company.

Preparing the candidate for a second round of interviews.

Describing the decision-making process and expected time frames.

Review the closing of the case study interview from Chapter 1 (repeated here). Does Marcia include all the elements of the closing? Answer the questions that follow.

Marcia:
Thank you for your directness. Now, do you have any questions for me?

Sara:
How soon will you be making a decision?

Marcia:
You are the last one that I will interview. I will be reviewing all of my interviews. I will make a decision by the end of the week.

Sara:

I am making $7 an hour as a temporary.

Marcia:

$7 is in our pay range. This position does come with benefits. I will give you a summary of our benefits to take with you. Anything else?

Sara:

No, I don't think so. I hope to hear from you.

Marcia:

You will, one way or the other. It's been nice talking to you, Sara. Thank you for coming in to see me.

1. What elements of the closing does Marcia include in her final comments to Sara?

   _____
   _____
   _____

2. Marcia does not sell the job or the company. Why do you think she omits this element?

   _____
   _____
   _____

3. Why is thanking the job candidate an important element of the closing?

   _____
   _____
   _____

4. When you are uncertain about the decision-making time frames, what should you do as a courtesy to your candidates?

   _____
   _____
   _____

5. Why does selling the company fall in the closing and not in the introduction?

   _____
   _____
   _____

CONSTRUCT YOUR PERSONAL INTERVIEW FORMAT

To construct your own format, write the statements or the questions that you might ask in most of your job interviews. Be sure to include questions you have found effective in getting the right information from your job candidates.

Introduction

Greeting: _____

_____

Body

Work: _____

_____

_____

Education: _____

_____

_____

Personal: _____

_____

_____

Closing

Questions: _____

_____

Sell: _____

_____

_____

Summary: _____

_____

_____

Note: The advantage of the interview format is that it provides consistency for all your interviews. Once you are proficient at using your interview format, you will be able to vary it to meet different interview situations.

EMPLOYMENT APPLICATION

General Information

Michaela Allen	*798-1223*
Name	Telephone
12 Arbor Way	*Receptonist/Secretery*
Address	Applying for
Milton, MD	
City/State	

Education

Milton High School	*Diploma*
High School, Trade	Degree or Certificate
Business or Vocational School	Degree or Certificate
College or University	Degree or Certificate
Graduate School	Degree or Certificate

Employment Experience

Employers: Start with your most recent employer.

Wilson Company	*Night Switchboard/Receptionist*
Company Name	Position
12 Ace Ave	*1/3/84*
Address	Start Date
Milton, MD	*6/30/92*
City/State	End Date
Mr. Finch	*Layoff*
Supervisor	Reason for Leaving
	Housewife
Company Name	Position
Address	Start Date
City/State	End Date
Supervisor	Reason for Leaving

Other

Organist at Church; Ladies Guild; Newsletter editor

Community Activities/Organizations

VARYING THE INTERVIEW FORMAT

Michaela Allen completes an application, as shown, for the receptionist/ secretary position.

When Marcia LaVoie welcomes Michaela to sit down for the interview, she observes that Michaela is about 45 or 46 years old. Marcia does not alter her introduction but she adapts the body of her interview to include these questions:

4

Job History

- What are your current job duties?

- How much receptionist activity is there at night?

- Whom do you provide typing for at night?

Community Interests

- What job skills have you used in working with the Ladies Guild?

- As the editor for the newsletter, what stories do you write?

1. Why does Marcia emphasize current job duties rather than obtain a job history?

_____

_____

_____

2. How will exploring Michaela's community service commitments build a better picture of Michaela?

_____

_____

_____

3. Are questions regarding education needed in this interview? If so, why would you include them?

_____

_____

_____

4. What other questions might you ask Michaela?

_____

_____

_____

5. Would you include selling the job and the company? Why or why not?

_____

_____

_____

INTERVIEW CONSIDERATIONS

Read the scenarios below and circle the area of experience—work, education, or personal—that you would concentrate on in the body of your interview to build a complete picture of each job candidate. The first one has been done for you.

Rita Vega has applied for a job in your department. She has been a housewife for the past 20 years. She has occasionally volunteered for school fund-raisers but has held no paying jobs.

Work   Education   (Personal)

John Qualler, who graduates from college in December, is applying for a job at your company. He is majoring in history and has a minor in biology. He has had two different summer jobs at a fast-food chain and at a country club in the kitchen. His extracurricular activities centered around photography.

Work   Education   Personal

Callie Lindroth is a mother on welfare who has just completed two job skills courses through job training programs—one for word processing and one in bookkeeping. She has a general education diploma (GED).

Work   Education   Personal

Ephraim Ezekiel, a retired engineer, wants a part-time security job at your company. He has two advanced degrees and 25 years' experience with a single company.

Work   Education   Personal

Chris Dromboski, who has just graduated from high school and has no job experience, is looking for entry-level work at your company. She decided not to go to college even though she had taken some honors courses and graduated near the top of her class.

Work   Education   Personal

H i n t s ──────────────────────────────────────

If You Interview Infrequently . . .

You will find that reviewing and rehearsing your established format will give you polish and confidence in conducting the interview.

4

Chapter Checkpoints

Use Your Interview Format Successfully

✓ Write and review your statements and questions before you interview.

✓ Practice your format with a colleague to get feedback.

✓ After several interviews, determine which questions give you the best information.

✓ Eliminate standard questions that give you no meaningful information.

5 | Questions? Questions!

This chapter will help you to:

- Create the best interview questions.
- Improve your probing techniques.
- Practice prescreening techniques.

WHAT KIND OF QUESTIONS SHOULD YOU ASK?

José Esposito, a manager of a fast-food restaurant, felt that if he got the right answers to his seven key questions, making an offer on the spot was the fastest way to get his new employee started. But some of his new employees were not meeting his expectations. Their interview answers were what he wanted, but their on-the-job performance did not meet his standards. ■

Here is José's list of key questions:

1. Do you like working with people?
2. Do you take pride in your appearance?
3. Are you accustomed to a varied work schedule?
4. Can you come to work at a moment's notice?
5. Are you generally neat and tidy?
6. Can you handle pressure?
7. Are you flexible about taking on different work assignments?

What are your observations about José's list of questions?

_____

_____

_____

Why do you think there is a difference between what the employees say in the interview and what they do on the job?

_____

_____

_____

How might you improve on José's list of questions?

_____

_____

THREE TYPES OF QUESTIONERS

Typically, questioners fall into three categories, based on the style of the questions they ask in an interview.

1. **The interrogator**—The interrogator asks specific questions that require a short, specific answer. These questions can usually be answered with a yes or no and produce terse, factual information about the job candidate. Interrogatory questions save you time by allowing you to get factual information quickly.

2. **The reporter**—The reporter asks questions that begin with *what, where, who, when, why,* or *how.* These questions encourage the candidate to respond with a lot of information. Reporter questions encourage the candidate to give details rather than a single-word answer.

3. **The prober**—The prober asks creative questions that use examples or suppositions to draw a more complete response from the job candidate. These questions, which look for reasons, behaviors, values, and patterns, also require the candidate to respond with more than a single word or simple phrase. They force the candidate to give thoughtful answers that reflect his or her values and motives.

The Interrogator

The list of José Esposito's questions at the beginning of the chapter was exclusively interrogatory. José's first question, "Do you like working with people?" is not particularly effective. Why?

_____

_____

_____

In the interview in Chapter 1, Marcia LaVoie, the hiring manager, asked Sara Anderson, "Are you still interested in discussing the position?" This question followed Marcia's clarification of the job for Sara. Why was it appropriate and effective?

_____

_____

_____

_____

Interrogatory questions are useful for discovering factual information. Which of the questions below elicit factual information? Circle Y if the question is factual. Circle N if the question is not factual.

Y   N   **1.** Are you going to college in the fall?

Y   N   **2.** Do you think you can do this job?

Y   N   **3.** Do you like your job at the shop?

Y   N   **4.** Can you lift 60 pounds?

Y   N   **5.** Did you handle accounts payable in your last job?

Y   N   **6.** Are you a fast learner?

Y   N   **7.** Did you get along with your supervisor?

Y   N   **8.** Have you ever worked a dictaphone?

Notice that the questions that do not solicit factual information (2, 3, 6, and 7) are opinion questions. Opinion questions prompt the candidate to tell the interviewer what the candidate wants to tell and not the actual facts.

The Reporter

Helen Dufour, who conducts many college campus interviews, finds that she loses interest in the interviews after about the fifth candidate. Although she uses open questions, which require more than yes or no answers, she wishes that she could be more interested in the interviews. ■

Here are the questions that she asks each college graduate:

1. What attracts you to our company?

2. What are your favorite courses in school?

3. What are your least favorite courses?

4. What are your grades?

5. What projects were you involved in during your classes?

6. What extracurricular activities do you participate in?

7. Where do you hope to be in 5 years? In 10 years?

Create five new reporter questions that use *why, how, where,* and *who* for Helen to use in her campus interviews.

1. _____

2. _____

3. _____

4. _____

5. _____

The Prober

The prober asks provoking questions that are difficult to create. They require some up-front thought and preparation. You may use several regularly in your interviews, or you may find that you create questions based on what the candidate says to you. Often, probing questions are tied directly to what experiences the candidate shares with you.

Melvin Lewis is interviewing someone involved in laying off staff after a merger. Some of his probing questions are directly related to the person's experience. ■

> You indicated that you had to lay off seven people. What did you do? How did you handle the aftershock with the staff that remained?

> As I listened to your description of the merger team, it struck me that you were receiving a lot of negative information about your company at the time. What were your feelings and how did you deal with them?

Here are some examples of probing questions. Think of probing questions of your own.

1. Please brag about yourself now, and tell me what your greatest accomplishments have been.
2. Identify five turning points in your career.
3. You are on several volunteer committees. How is leading volunteers different from leading employees at work?

PRESCREENING INTERVIEW

Bernard Cahn is looking for a part-time bookkeeper. He has selected 10 candidates who responded to his ad. Since he doesn't want to waste time interviewing, he plans to call each person he selected and prescreen them on the telephone. He has completed his must-have worksheet and is ready to begin. ■

PRESCREENING INTERVIEW

Here are 14 questions and answers from his first prescreening interview with Janice Lahey. Answer the questions that follow them.

1. Q: "Janice, I am calling because you sent in your résumé for the part-time bookkeeper job. I just want to ask you some questions to see if you match our job and if it's what you want. Do you have a few minutes?"
A: "Yes, I do."

2. Q: "Janice, from your résumé, it looks like you are doing some bookkeeping right now. Is that right?"
A: "Well, yes. I work in accounting right now."

3. Q: "Do you handle accounts receivables?"
A: "Yes, that's the main part of my job."

4. Q: "How about accounts payables?"
A: "I don't handle payables in this job. I did that when I worked at the creamery four years ago."

5. Q: "What kind of reports do you work with?"
A: "Well, I work with aging reports mostly. I have to report on all 30, 60, and 90 accounts. And I produce monthly income reports for my boss."

6. Q: "Do you have any experience with LOTUS?"
A: "Yes."

7. Q: "Okay. You're working full-time now?"
   A: "Yes."

8. Q: "Why are you interested in a part-time job?"
   A: "Well, I want to spend more time with my kids. I miss all the school activities with a 40-hour job."

9. Q: "How old are your kids?"
   A: "Both are in middle school. They are a year apart."

10. Q: "Are they sick much?"
   A: "No, they rarely miss school. And I'm never sick."

11. Q: "Okay. There's just one more thing. This is a 25-hour-a-week job. You can pretty much pick your hours, except Mondays. You have to be here from 8:00 to 1:00 for our home office reports. Is that okay?"
   A: "That is fine with me. I applied because the ad said flexible hours."

12. Q: "Good. Sounds like you have what I'm looking for. Do you have any questions?"
   A: "Well, yes. What is the salary?"

13. Q: "I'm looking to pay between $6 and $8 an hour, depending on experience."
   A: "I see. Well, those figures are less than what I make right now. I would really like $10 an hour."

14. Q: "Mmmmm. I'm not prepared to pay that, but I will think about it. If I decide I can swing that, I will call you to come in for an interview."
   A: "Thank you. I'd appreciate that."

1. Critique Bernard's overall interview with Janice.

_____

_____

_____

_____

2. Reduce the number of questions Bernard asked by improving questions 2, 3, 4, 5, 6, and 8.

_____

_____

_____

_____

3. Bernard was sidetracked by Janice's reason for wanting a part-time job. Were his questions proper? What would have been a better follow-up to her response?

_____

_____

_____

_____

4. The purpose of a prescreening interview is to save time. What should Bernard have asked as one of his opening questions?

_____

_____

_____

_____

5

Review & Practice

Rewrite and improve these often-asked questions.

1. Do you like working with people?

_____

_____

2. What are your weaknesses?

_____

_____

3. Are you a fast learner?

_____

_____

4. In your opinion, which is more difficult, management or technical work?

_____

_____

5. Why did you leave your job?

_____

_____

6. Are you a team player?

_____

_____

7. Are you an organized person?

_____

_____

8. How well do you handle pressure?

_____

_____

9. What kind of supervision do you prefer?

_____

_____

10. What was your favorite subject in school?

_____

_____

5

Chapter Checkpoints

Improve Your Questions

✓ Make your fact-finding questions choice questions:

"Do you prefer working with a group or working alone?"

"Will you need more training for this job, or has your coursework prepared you sufficiently?"

✓ Avoid negative questions that invite agreement rather than discover the candidate's real feelings:

Instead of: "Isn't filing the most boring part of the job?"

Ask: "How do you react to routine parts of your job?"

✓ Make open questions plural:

"What are (not *is*) some of your achievements?"

"What are your best skills?"

✓ Adjust your prepared questions in response to examples the job candidate offers:

"I heard you say that you opened the travel agency in the morning. One of the duties of this position is to open the office and let employees into the building. How did Mrs. Caldwell rate your reliability in this area?"

CHAPTER

6 | Conducting the Interview

This chapter will help you to:

- Improve your interview poise.
- Use effective listening skills.
- Present a positive image to all job candidates.

30-SECOND IMPRESSION

It is said that we make a lasting impression on other persons within the first 30 seconds of meeting them. Read and rate your 30-second impression of the following interviewers. Use the rating scale that follows the descriptions.

Michael Smith is on the phone with his feet atop a desk littered with papers and folders of various sizes and descriptions. A cold cup of coffee sits on the edge of his desk near a filled ashtray. He squints at Dave Mead, his interview appointment who is standing in the doorway, and waves him to come in and take a seat. ■

Joyce Bellair approaches Luanne Retton, who is hanging up her coat in the foyer closet, with these words: "Welcome! You must be Luanne." Joyce takes a sip from the coffee cup she is holding in her hand. "Come on in. We'll go to my office. How about a nice cup of coffee or tea before we start?" ■

Brian Washington, who arrived punctually for his appointment, has been waiting for 15 minutes in the lobby before Maureen Toomey comes out to meet him. She is impeccably dressed in a tailored suit and shakes his hand as he stands up. "Brian, so good to meet you. Won't you come with me to our conference room?" She turns and leads him down the corridor. ■

Rex Peterson comes out from behind the counter to meet Cindy Carlsberg, who is an applicant for a hostess position. He plunks a soiled apron on the counter and says, "Hello, Cindy. Let's sit over there in one of the booths. Sorry about my appearance. We're a little shorthanded in the kitchen today." He sighs as he brushes some crumbs from the booth seats. ■

Rating Scale: 1 - - - - - 5 - - - - - 10
                      Poor   **Good**   **Excellent**

Michael Smith   Rating Score: _____
    Critique _____
    _____
    _____

Joyce Bellair   Rating Score: _____
    Critique _____
    _____
    _____

Maureen Toomey   Rating Score: _____
    Critique _____
    _____
    _____

Rex Peterson   Rating Score: _____
    Critique _____
    _____
    _____

SETTING THE TONE

At the opening handshake, you:

- Set the tone for the rest of the interview.
- Establish rapport with your job candidate and potential employee.
- Represent your company to the candidate.
- Display your company's values and attitude toward its people.

What are the first three things you do to set the tone for your interviews?

1. _____

2. _____

3. _____

THE INTERVIEW SPACE

Interview space is part of your interview. It can relax or distract your job candidate. It can create an open environment, or it can place barriers between you and your candidate.

Select the award title for the following space descriptions: most favorable, least favorable, most open, most threatening, most distracting, most cordial.

Descriptions	Your Award Title
1. Private office. Interviewer behind desk. Candidate in chair in front of desk.	_____
2. Open floor. Interviewer at desk in corner. Chair at side of desk for candidate.	_____
3. Conference room. Interviewer sits across conference table from candidate.	_____
4. Table in closed restaurant section. Interviewer sits across table from candidate. Coffee on table.	_____
5. Lobby of building. Interviewee sits next to candidate on couch.	_____
6. No office. Tour building side-by-side while conducting interview.	_____

Now select the award title for your interview space.

Description	Your Award Title
_____	_____
_____	

What does it need for improvement? _____

_____

_____

The key to a favorable interview space is that it be free from distractions and disruptions. Without distractions and disruptions, you can create privacy in almost any setting.

Assess and Rate Your Interview Opening and Setting

Use the following rating scale to determine your personal score in presenting an open welcome and creating 30-second rapport.

Rating Scale: **1 - - - - - -5 - - - - - -10**
                      Never   Mostly   Always

Personal Statement	Rating
1. I clear my desk and prepare for each interview at least five minutes in advance.	__
2. I know the job candidate's name and use it when I greet him or her.	__
3. I am groomed according to company standards.	__
4. I give a firm handshake, look the candidate in the eye, and smile during my greeting.	__
5. I make sure that I will have no phone calls or disruptions during the interview.	__
6. The area where I interview is clean and makes a good impression.	__
7. There are no outside distractions.	__
8. If there are any disruptions or distractions over which I have no control, I alert the candidate to them (for example, a company fire drill).	__
9. I make sure my job candidate is comfortable before I begin the interview.	__
10. I begin the interview after the welcome and clarify what the interview is about and what I hope to accomplish.	__
Rating Total	__

If your score is in the 10 to 30 range: Improve, Improve, Improve.

If your score is in the 40 to 70 range: Better and Better.

If your score is in the 80 to 100 range: Congratulations!

> ## Hints
>
> Each assessment item describes an action that you can incorporate into your interview routine. Improve your score and improve your interview image.

A CASE OF IDENTITY

Alexander Tarkoff was pleased by the response to his ad for a shipping and receiving clerk. To date he had interviewed 25 candidates. From the 25, Alexander narrowed the field to 12 potential candidates. He gave the 13 résumés with *No* penciled on the top of each résumé to his secretary for letters. As he reviewed the remaining 12 résumés with *OK* penciled on them, he found that he was having trouble remembering who was who. ∎

"Cheryl," he called out. "Do you remember what Roger Dumont looked like?"

"Wasn't he the one with the beard?"

"No, that was Wednesday. His name was Clinton."

"Oh, that's right. Dumont? Was he Monday?"

"Yes. At 9 o'clock."

"Umm. Was he the short one who drove the Mustang?"

"Right. Thanks."

1. Alexander's discomfort at taking notes during an interview will cause what problems in making a hiring decision based on these interviews?

   _____

   _____

   _____

2. What do you recommend Alexander do before he makes an offer to one of the candidates?

   _____

   _____

   _____

3. What is the long-term solution to Alexander's dilemma about remembering his interview candidates?

_____

_____

_____

4. Does Alexander's poor memory of some of the job candidates indicate that he is a poor listener? What other factors hamper memory?

_____

_____

_____

The best questions in the world are useless unless you have fine-tuned your listening skills. Not only must you *hear* what is said but you must *listen* to the way in which it is said. Experienced interviewers advise to listen for a change in the tenor of the speaker's voice. You will find that the tone may drop or voice tense up when the person is trying to describe a stressful or unpleasant situation or person.

Here are three listening techniques, with examples from the Chapter 1 case study, to help you probe when you hear a tone change or when the person becomes visibly uncomfortable in describing a work event or interpersonal conflict:

1. Paraphrasing—You restate in your own words your understanding of what the person has just said.

Marcia:

If I understand you correctly, your dress style was more suited to, say, going out with your friends than going to work?

Sara:

That's right. My clothes were neat and trendy but not for business.

2. Reflection—You respond to show that you understand the facts and the feelings behind the facts.

Sara:

The people at the other company were more status-oriented. If your job wasn't important, neither were you. I didn't like that.

Marcia:

I don't blame you. I wouldn't want to feel that what I did wasn't important. Were you treated that way by everyone in the company?

3. Clarification—You probe to get information that makes what the person is saying clearer to the discussion.

Sara:

. . . I like numbers. I think I would want something to do with accounting.

Marcia:

That's interesting. I don't think I heard you mention accounting in any of your positions. Did you work with numbers in any of these jobs?

Write your listening response to each of the following, and identify which listening technique you will use to respond.

1. "I got along okay with my supervisor. Of course, we didn't always see eye-to-eye. But then nobody does all the time, do they?"

Listening Technique: _____

Your Response: _____

_____

2. "It was a very confusing job. I had two—no, three—bosses. I typed for Ron and took messages for the three men in the lab. I didn't type their reports. There was another secretary who did that. And sometimes I ordered supplies for the whole office."

Listening Technique: _____

Your Response: _____

_____

3. "I was very embarrassed. She yelled at me in front of a whole group of customers. There was nothing I could do about the machine jam; it happened to everyone who worked that counter. The next day, I gave my notice. I just couldn't face going to work there again."

Listening Technique: _____

Your Response: _____

_____

SAVE THE SELLING FOR LAST

Marcia LaVoie, our hiring manager, is obviously impressed with Tracy Callum, who has three years of experience at a job very similar to the receptionist/secretary position that Marcia supervises. She tells Tracy, "Based on what you told me, I think our job here is almost identical to your last job. Your responsibilities would include the same duties: greeting visitors, directing calls, and a variety of secretarial projects. Here, however, you would not have to work on Saturdays. I think that is probably a plus for you."

Marcia encourages Tracy to respond. Tracy seems genuinely enthusiastic about the job opportunity. Marcia continues to tell Tracy about the company: "I think you will find everyone here very friendly and cooperative. It is a fairly relaxed atmosphere. Everyone calls each other by his or her first name, including the president. We even have a company lunch every quarter where we order out and the food is brought in. And we all have a good time."

Marcia also reviews the benefits package with Tracy and points out that she will have some benefits that she did not enjoy in her last job. ∎

In making her sales pitch, Marcia follows these guidelines:

1. Listen to what the candidate feels is important to his or her well-being and success.
2. Identify parts of your job that interest or fit the candidate's experience and expectations.
3. Describe the company environment and the people who will work with the candidate.
4. Compare company plans or programs that are special or that are superior to the candidate's current or past situation.
5. Conclude with a warm thank-you.

Two Schools of Thought

Two schools of thought exist concerning to whom you should make your sales pitch:

1. To the top candidates only.
2. To all the candidates.

Marcia LaVoie adheres to the first school of thought: sell to the top candidate(s) only.

1. What are the advantages/disadvantages of selling to the top candidates only?

Advantages: _____

_____

_____

Disadvantages: _____

_____

_____

2. Which school of thought do you belong to? Why?

_____

_____

_____

3. Write the things you include in your sales pitch to your job candidates.

_____

_____

_____

THE BOTTOM LINE: MAKE YOUR INTERVIEWS THE BEST

Now that you've had a chance to digest a great deal of information about all the steps in the interview process, take a minute to sit back and read through the list below. Keep this list as your interview "crib sheet"—these are the most important techniques guaranteed to make each interview a success. If you read this list before every interview you conduct, you're sure to hire the best.

Interview Checklist

Put the candidate at ease. Start the interview with easy questions.

Listen carefully to the way in which candidates answer the questions.

Explore the whys behind what happened to a candidate.

Withhold judgment until the interview is complete.

Take notes to aid your memory and judgment.

Look for patterns of behavior in a candidate's job history.

Refer to your list of questions to make certain that you get all the answers you wanted.

(*continued*)

Interview Checklist (*concluded*)

Take time to observe the candidate's expressions and listen for vocal tone changes.

Tell the truth about the job and the company.

Sell your company to all candidates.

Avoid assumptions about the candidate based on his or her appearance, education, life-style, or past employer.

Let your candidate speak freely and avoid putting words in his or her mouth.

Limit the time spent verifying the résumé data.

Avoid belittling or reprimanding candidates because you do not agree with them or hold their beliefs.

Schedule appointments carefully so that you are not rushed in the interview process.

Give the candidate time to talk.

Be careful of making promises or guarantees about salary, benefits, or job responsibilities.

Concentrate on relevant information.

Avoid telegraphing the right answers to the candidate.

Be aware of discriminatory questions and your biases.

Chapter Checkpoints

Conducting the Interview

✓ Let the candidate present his or her credentials first.

✓ Ensure that you get all the information you need.

✓ Save the sales pitch for last.

✓ Take complete notes.

✓ Eliminate distractions and disruptions.

✓ Never make assumptions based on a person's appearance.

7 | Rating and Ranking

This chapter will help you to:

- Reevaluate your selection process if needed.
- Select a candidate based on your objective and subjective data.
- Rethink your selection when your first choice turns you down.
- Ask for references.

WHEN YOUR SELECTION PROCESS IS FAULTY

When your newly hired employee does not do the following, your selection process may be at fault:

Stay for more than three months.

Perform as you expected.

Like the job.

Fit in with the rest of the employees.

When your selection process is at fault, you may have:

1. Allowed the candidate's warm personality to overshadow his or her job skill weaknesses.
2. Failed to obtain enough objective data to make a good decision.
3. Hired a person for his or her potential rather than for the job.
4. Made some assumptions about the person based on his or her appearance and not on interview answers.

SELECTION SHORTHAND

Improve your selection process by creating an interview summary chart that allows you to look at a "snapshot" of each candidate in relation to your job criteria.

Your interview summary chart should:

- List the names of the job candidates you are considering for the position.
- Display the job criteria (must-haves) with a separate column for each candidate's summary.
- Provide for your evaluation of the candidate's personal qualities and your reaction to the candidate.
- Provide for comments on the candidate's goals.

Using your interview summary chart will help you avoid selection mistakes and force you to critique each candidate.

Once you have completed your summary chart, you may want to rank each candidate. This is useful should your first selection turn down your job offer.

Look at the interview summary chart that Marcia LaVoie completed after she finished her interviews.

Marcia wrote her must-haves under "Job Criteria" and her reactions under "Personal Qualities" and "Goals."

MARCIA'S INTERVIEW SUMMARY CHART

Interview Summary Chart for: Receptionist/Secretary							Date: 9/92
	Job Criteria						
Job Candidate	Switchboard (6 Months)	Greet Public	Details	Typing	Office 1–2 Years	Personal Qualities	Goals
Tracy Callum #1	3 years Receptionist/ secretary	Yes	Yes	Same as ours	5 years	Pleasant, works unsupervised OK + +	Same type of job
Sara Anderson	1 year Travel	Yes	Yes	School, some secretarial	2 years	Friendly, some immaturity OK +	Executive secretary

MARCIA'S INTERVIEW SUMMARY CHART (*concluded*)

Interview Summary Chart for: Receptionist/Secretary   **Date: 9/92**

Job Candidate	Switchboard (6 Months)	Greet Public	Details	Typing	Office 1–2 Years	Personal Qualities	Goals
						Job Criteria	
Martha Wagstaff	2 years	So-so Waitress	Maybe	Little experience	2 + years	Abrupt OK –	No goals
Michaela Allen	8 years	Yes	Don't know	Light typing (spelling)	8 years	Pleasant, mature OK + +	Good job security

Marcia combined her chart analysis with her reactions and decided to offer the job to Tracy, her top candidate. Marcia did not rank her other candidates.

Using the chart, rank the remaining three candidates based on Marcia's information. Use number 2 for your second choice, number 3 for your third choice, and number 4 for your last choice.

Create your own interview summary chart using your must-have chart for job criteria.

7

Interview Summary Chart for: _____		Date: _____
Job Candidate	Job Criteria	Personal Qualities	Goals

WHEN NUMBER ONE SAYS NO

"Tom, I'm really frustrated," Marcia sighed as she tossed her interview summary chart on Tom Boland's desk. "My top candidate for the receptionist position turned me down, and I am not sure whom I should I hire instead."

Her boss Tom looked over the chart and replied, "It looks like it's between Sara and Michaela."

"That's right. One has too much secretarial experience and the other not enough. Maybe I should just toss a coin."

"I don't think that's the answer," said Tom. "Let me give you some advice." ∎

When your first choice turns you down and your second and third candidates are not exact matches, follow Tom's advice to Marcia:

1. Review your job for its essential job duties.
2. Identify your number one must-have credential.

3. Identify job skills that can be learned in a short period of time.

4. Determine what kind of training support you have available.

5. Review your candidates in light of their ability to learn.

6. Identify the candidate's personal goals and their impact on how long the candidate will stay in the job.

The Second Choice

Use Tom's advice and help Marcia select a receptionist/secretary.

Interview Summary Chart for: **Receptionist/Secretary**						Date: **9/92**	
	Job Criteria						
Job Candidate	**Switchboard (6 Months)**	**Greet Public**	**Details**	**Typing**	**Office 1–2 Years**	**Personal Qualities**	**Goals**
Sara Anderson	1 year Travel	Yes	Yes	School, some secretarial	2 years	Friendly, some immaturity OK +	Executive secretary
Michaela Allen	8 years	Yes	Don't know	Light typing (spelling)	8 years	Pleasant, mature OK + +	Good job security

1. The number one must-have is: _____

_____

2. The job skill(s) that can be learned quickly: _____

_____

3. Sandy, the current receptionist, is available for one week of overlap training. She can train the new hire to: _____

_____

4. Marcia did not explore how any of the candidates learned. Based on the candidates' summaries, can you make any inferences about their learning ability? If so, what?

_____

_____

5. Which candidate will stay in the job longer, based on her expressed personal goal?

_____

You would make the job offer to: _____

Why? _____

CHECKING REFERENCES

Fill in the blanks.

1. Checking references is very important because _____
_____
_____.

2. Checking references is a waste of time because _____
_____
_____.

Whatever your opinion or practice, references provide an opportunity to *confirm* facts and, in some cases, inferences.

Because of litigation fears, many employers limit the amount of information they offer when you call for a reference on a past employee. In spite of the fact that you may receive only limited information, the reference call at its barest can:

Confirm a candidate's employment dates.

Confirm a candidate's job title and reason for termination.

Confirm a candidate's ending salary amount or level.

Confirm a candidate's rehire eligibility.

Open Reference Call

In cases where your job candidate has granted oral or written permission for his or her past employer to give a reference, be prepared to ask pertinent questions.

Reference Questionnaire

1. What was your work relationship to (name)? _____
_____

2. How long did you work with (name)? _____
_____

(*continued*)

Reference Questionnaire (*concluded*)

3. How would you describe his or her work habits? _____
_____
_____

4. How was (name) viewed by his or her peers (boss, customers, and co-workers)? _____
_____
_____

5. Rate his or her attendance and punctuality habits. _____
_____
_____

6. What were his or her strengths? _____
_____
_____

7. What were his or her weaknesses (or areas for development)? _____
_____
_____
_____

8. What else can you tell me about (name)? _____
_____
_____

7

IS YOUR SELECTION PROCESS AT FAULT?

The real test of your selection skills is the performance of your new employee on the job. The following exercise contains examples of what can happen after an employee is hired.

Circle Y if you think the interviewer should have anticipated this problem from the interview. Circle N if you think the interviewer could not have discovered this in the interview. For each Y that you circle, jot down what the interviewer should have discovered.

Y   N   1. Sonya, the new receptionist, is very pleasant but continually mixes up messages left for the managers.

_____
_____

Y N   **2.** Steven, the new warehouser, is laid up with a bad back after a fall.

_____

_____

Y N   **3.** Louis, the new busboy, was late for work six times in the first month.

_____

_____

Y N   **4.** Marlene, after two weeks, left her job as district manager. She said the job was not what she expected.

_____

_____

Y N   **5.** Avi, the new chemist, reported to the nurse that he has allergies and may not be able to continue to work at the lab.

_____

_____

Y N   **6.** Max, the new electrician, has not shown up for work for three days and cannot be reached.

_____

_____

Y N   **7.** Lily, a three-month teller, is bored and restless on the job.

_____

_____

Y N   **8.** Andrew has been moody since he started. One day he's up; the next day he's down.

_____

_____

Grade Raoul's Selection

Raoul Garcia is the manager at a distribution warehouse. When he took over the management responsibility, he had to clean up a very lax operation. Since the beginning of the year, he has hired nine new employees. It is now December and his boss wants to discuss his performance results with him. One of the areas they will be discussing is how well Raoul's new people are working out. ■

Raoul jotted down notes about each person he hired:

Six Who Are Still Employed:

JS	Start 1/3	Three months: So-so. Annual review: Much improved. Gets along with all. Raise OK.
RB	Start 5/4	Three months: Super. Annual review: Expected to continue. Seen as leader. Give more duties. Increase, too.
FK	Start 7/1	Three months: OK. Annual review: Will be OK. Punctual and reliable. Accepted by all.
ML	Start 7/15	Three months: OK. Annual review: OK. Some attendance issues. A bit feisty. Has temper.
KK	Start 10/31	Three months: May terminate. Not working out. Bad apple. Everyone avoids him. (Annual review not applicable at this time.)
SD	Start 11/1	Three months: Seems very eager. Good attitude. Good attendance and appearance. (Annual review not applicable at this time.)

Three Who Are No Longer Employed:

WW	Never showed up to work in January.
AM	Transfer from purchasing in March. Retransferred in April. Too snotty.
GL	Excellent worker. Hired in January. Unexpected return to school in September. Maybe school vacations?

Complete the following chart to rate Raoul's new hires. Include all nine employees. Note: You may not have enough information to fill in all the columns for each employee. JS has been completed for you.

Use the following numbers for rating employee performance:
1—Unsatisfactory   2—Need Improvement   3—Competent
4—Outstanding

SELECTION REPORT CARD

Name	Still Employed	Three-Month Performance Rating	Annual Performance Rating	Peer Acceptance	Employee Rating
JS	Yes	So-so	Improved	Good	3

Like Raoul, all managers seek to have their new hires stay beyond three months and become fully competent by their annual review. Based on these criteria, how would you rate Raoul, and how can Raoul improve his selection report card?

_____

_____

_____

Chapter Checkpoints

How Are Your Hiring Skills?

The results of successful selection are that your new employee:

✓ Performs the job skillfully.

✓ Enjoys the challenge of the job.

✓ Works well with other employees.

✓ Stays and grows with your company.

Selection Tips

✓ Review your successful hires and determine what you did right in the hiring process.

✓ Reflect on your new employee's progress and behavior to discover if you missed obtaining information in your original interview.

✓ Reevaluate your interview questions and format for missing probes.

✓ Reward yourself and your new employee when things work out well for both of you.

Post-Test

Circle the letter that best completes each statement.

1. When you have a job opening, you should identify:
   a. The essential job skills needed for the job.
   b. The purpose of the job and the main tasks.
   c. The needed personal attributes and preferred skills.
   d. All of the above.

2. When you review applications or résumés, you should:
   a. Ignore spelling errors and typos.
   b. Look for gaps between employment dates or frequent job changes.
   c. Check to see if you know any of the references listed.
   d. Sort them in alphabetical order to save time.

3. Because of laws that forbid discrimination in hiring, you cannot ask:
   a. Why the candidate left his or her last job.
   b. How well the candidate gets along with persons of authority.
   c. If the candidate can perform the job as described by the interviewer.
   d. Where the candidate grew up and now lives.

4. The Americans with Disabilities Act restricts hiring managers from asking:
   a. How the candidate became disabled.
   b. If the candidate was a Vietnam-era veteran.
   c. If the candidate has schedule conflicts.
   d. If the candidate can perform the job as described by the interviewer.

5. One method that helps interviewers avoid asking questions that might be construed as discriminatory is:
   a. To ask only interrogatory questions.

b. To ask questions that confirm the information on the application/résumé.

c. To prepare and test questions in advance of the interview.

d. To listen without making any comments.

6. By creating your own interview format, you can:

a. Control the flow of talk in the interview.

b. Sell the position at the beginning of the interview.

c. Get the candidate to tell you about any personal problems.

d. Prevent the candidate from wasting your time.

7. In closing your interview with the candidate, make sure you:

a. Tell the candidate whether or not he or she has the job.

b. Describe the decision-making process.

c. Sell the job only if the candidate indicates interest.

d. Give the candidate a complete tour of your facility.

8. In the interview, reporter questions:

a. Can usually be answered with a yes or no.

b. Are creative and draw more complex responses from the candidate.

c. Begin with *what, where, who, when, why* or *how.*

d. Are used to get terse factual information quickly.

9. The most favorable setting for an interview is:

a. A private office with comfortable chairs.

b. Free from distractions and disruptions.

c. A conference room with windows.

d. After office hours to avoid telephone interruptions.

10. The purpose of taking notes in the interview is to:

a. Keep you from becoming bored in the interview.

b. Show the candidate that you are interested.

     c. Relieve the candidate's initial tension.

     d. Assist you in recalling the details of each interview.

11. As one of the listening techniques, clarification is used to

     a. Restate in your own words your understanding of what the person has said.

     b. Show you understand the facts and the feelings behind the facts.

     c. Get information that makes what the person is saying clearer to the discussion.

     d. All of the above.

12. In making your sales pitch for your job and your company, you want to:

     a. Identify parts of the job that interest or fit the candidate's experience or expectations.

     b. Promise to give the candidate special benefits if he or she accepts the job.

     c. Avoid discussing the company environment and culture.

     d. Brag about how much better your salary and benefits programs are compared to the candidate's former company.

13. Your selection process may be at fault if:

     a. None of the candidates accept your job offer.

     b. Your new employee outperforms your expectations.

     c. Your new employee does not stay for more than three months.

     d. References lied to you about the candidate.

14. Your selection process is successful if your new employee:

     a. Performs the job skillfully.

     b. Works well with other employees.

     c. Enjoys the challenge of the job.

     d. Does all of the above.

15. When developing your questions, you should:

    a. Never ask a question that is answered by yes or no.

    b. Ask only probing questions.

    c. Save time by asking questions that give you only factual answers.

    d. Use interrogatory questions to obtain pertinent facts or to confirm specific details.

THE BUSINESS SKILLS EXPRESS SERIES

This growing series of books addresses a broad range of key business skills and topics to meet the needs of employees, human resource departments, and training consultants.

To obtain information about these and other Business Skills Express books, please call Business One IRWIN toll free at: 1-800-634-3966.

Effective Performance Management	ISBN	1-55623-867-3
Hiring the Best	ISBN	1-55623-865-7
Writing that Works	ISBN	1-55623-856-8
Customer Service Excellence	ISBN	1-55623-969-6
Writing for Business Results	ISBN	1-55623-854-1
Powerful Presentation Skills	ISBN	1-55623-870-3
Meetings that Work	ISBN	1-55623-866-5
Effective Teamwork	ISBN	1-55623-880-0
Time Management	ISBN	1-55623-888-6
Assertiveness Skills	ISBN	1-55623-857-6
Motivation at Work	ISBN	1-55623-868-1
Overcoming Anxiety at Work	ISBN	1-55623-869-X
Positive Politics at Work	ISBN	1-55623-879-7
Telephone Skills at Work	ISBN	1-55623-858-4
Managing Conflict at Work	ISBN	1-55623-890-8
The New Supervisor: Skills for Success	ISBN	1-55623-762-6
The *Americans with Disabilities Act:* What Supervisors Need to Know	ISBN	1-55623-889-4